D0118707

How to be a Goddess

How to be a Goddess

Ancient Wisdom for Modern Women

Valerie Khoo

Red Wheel
Boston, MA / York Beach, ME

Contents

Introduction

You've seen her. The gorgeous woman who turns heads whenever she walks into a room, or the friend who always exudes an air of confidence and optimism. Or perhaps you have a work colleague who manages to pull together projects with professionalism and panache. Or an aunt or sister who simply oozes warmth, happiness and love.

We all admire different qualities in other people, but there are some women we all notice – women who have an intangible self-assurance and glow that seem to radiate from within. These women are modern-day goddesses. And the good news is that each and every one of us has the power to bring our inner goddess to the forefront.

Success, happiness and an abundant life are all possible – if you nurture your unique gifts and talents, design a life worth living, and approach it all with the kind of practical attitude that will turn your dreams into reality.

To achieve what you want out of life involves developing your natural instincts and letting your inner goddess shine. This isn't a new concept; it's an approach that the goddesses of yesteryear pioneered way before we were ever around. And it's from these inspirational goddesses that we can learn how to harness our own innate powers and allow our intuition to guide us in life.

The myths surrounding the Greek goddesses have mesmerized the world for centuries. These tales, covering everything from love and beauty to treachery and determination, are enthralling, exciting and entertaining. But the stories are more than just ancient Greece's answer to daytime soap operas.

The sagas, and the mythical goddesses who star in them – Athena, Demeter, Persephone, Aphrodite, Artemis, and Hestia – are still looked upon in today's world as key elements of history. These goddesses were all beautiful and powerful, and they influenced lives and made an impact on the world around them.

But this book is not about goddess worship. Far from it. It's about drawing inspiration from these women of ancient times and applying it to your life today.

It's also about being inspired by the goddesses in your own life – your friends, family and mentors – and allowing your own gorgeous inner goddess to emerge. This applies to all areas of life, from love and happiness to career and money. If you're guided by your own unique values and motivated by other inspirational women, creating a life that is fulfilling, happy and truly magnificent is not only possible, it's simply waiting to happen.

Inspirational Goddesses

HOW ARE GREEK MYTHS RELEVANT TO ME?

So you're reading this book on how to be a gorgeous goddess – but you're not quite sure what a bunch of women from the past, in flowing dresses, will be able to offer a 21st century girl whose only exposure to Greek myths was history class in high school.

The Greek goddesses Athena, Demeter, Persephone, Aphrodite, Artemis, and Hestia have a lot more clout than most people give them credit for. Sure, they have exotic names and have all been immortalized in poems and stories that have lasted generations. But their influence can be much more far-reaching – and personal.

Modern-day goddesses don't live in the past – just as you don't – but they do know that the only way to move forward with confidence is to learn from experience and take advantage of inspirational role models who can offer advice or guidance in various aspects of life.

Think about how some of the women in your life have shaped you. Think of the warmth and kindness of a loving grandmother; the guidance of a kick-ass female boss who's shown you how to succeed with style; or perhaps the loyalty of a best friend.

This kind of informal female nurturing and mentoring goes on all the time. Some people may ask why we should bother with ancient Greek myths when today's women are able to motivate and inspire us. The reality is that not all of us are blessed with a bunch of go-getting women who are prepared to be our own personal cheer squad. And even if we're lucky enough to have wonderful women in our lives whom we can call on for advice, they can't be there for us all the time – they have their own lives to lead.

If you have a good look at the mythical Greek goddesses, you will discover attitudes and characteristics that are universal and constant. Combining your own outlook on life with inspiration from each goddess' unique personality, you can nurture a winning attitude that will help you grab life with both hands and steer it in the direction of your dreams.

Aphrodite

Artemis

Hestia

Remember, though, that this book is about how you can be a goddess – it's not an instructional manual on how you can become the next Athena or Artemis.

Let's discover a few powerful women who offer advice that has stood the test of time. Let's meet the ancient goddesses who will help you turn your 21st century world into one full of excitement, success and happiness …

Athena was a gorgeous goddess who exuded strength, wisdom and creativity. Tradesmen, such as blacksmiths and potters, celebrated her as their patron. Women also believed her to be the patron of cooking, weaving and spinning. So Athena was not only deeply practical, she was also full of creativity and inspiration.

As the daughter of Zeus, she was also the protectress of Athens. This means many thought of her as a warrior queen – she is often pictured with a sword and shield. Think of her as ancient Greece's answer to Lara Croft. Ancient military forces used her as their inspiration in times of battle. However, even though Athena's strength motivated many warring armies, it's her wisdom in mediation and interpreting the law that really resolved conflicts.

The lore of Athena includes a beautiful myth about how she won a contest against Poseidon, lord of the seas. The gods decreed that the winner would be the one who presented the most useful gift to everyone on earth. Poseidon first offered the sea, and followed up with a wild and powerful horse, an animal often associated with war.

Athena offered something quite different: she struck the earth with her sword, and from that place the first olive tree emerged – the tree produced oil which people could use for burning lamps, cooking, and anointing their bodies. A branch from the olive tree also became a symbol of peace.

The gods knew that a peaceful offering was far better than one that encouraged battle, and they declared her the winner. Clearly, Athena was powerful and astute, but she also embodied compassion, relied on feminine intuition and nurtured creativity.

 Athena sprang fully grown from the head of her father Zeus

As Zeus' favorite child, she become his friend and confidant

 Athena had a love of art, and also taught crafts and created musical instruments

She was one of the three virgin goddesses and radiated light and brilliance

11

Demeter and Persephone

The stories of Demeter and Persephone are inextricably intertwined. As mother and daughter, their tale is one of rebirth, temptation and boundless love. And just like the dilemmas we face in today's world, this ancient myth deals with the constantly changing seasons of life and the inevitable struggle between darkness and light.

Demeter was the goddess of the fertile earth and mother to Persephone, who was considered the maiden of spring. At the time, the earth was abundant with fruit and soil and there was no winter. One day Persephone was abducted by Hades, the god of the underworld. Demeter searched everywhere for her beautiful daughter, and was so overcome with grief that crops withered and the earth became dry and barren.

When Zeus saw this disaster he urged Hades to return Persephone to her mother. Although Hades agreed, he encouraged Persephone to eat some pomegranate seeds before she returned to earth. Hades knew that if Persephone ate any food from the underworld it would tie her to the place forever.

As a result of eating only three pomegranate seeds, Persephone was able to live with her mother in the light of the world for nine months of the year, and during that time the earth was rich in food and life. But she was also destined to spend three months a year as queen of the underworld – this was the earth's winter.

Demeter was also known as the goddess of grain and the harvest, as she gave people the gift of corn, which they could store for the cold months. Even though Persephone was an innocent and vulnerable maiden, subjected to difficult trials and challenges, she was ultimately able to deal with life's blows and transform into a woman of awareness and strength.

Persephone

 Persephone was picking a narcissus flower when Hades took her into the underworld

 When Demeter and her daughter were together, birds sang, flowers bloomed and the earth overflowed with abundance

Demeter

 Demeter is the sister of Zeus, Hades and Poseidon – the three brothers who ruled heaven, the underworld and the sea respectively

13

APHRODITE

One of the most famous Greek goddesses, Aphrodite was the goddess of love and beauty. She was passionate and powerful, inspiring love and lust among men and gods. Aphrodite certainly didn't have any problems getting attention or encouraging desire among her admirers.

If Aphrodite were around today, she'd be right at home with the glitz and glamor of Hollywood. While some people may envy this kind of charisma and pulling power, it's also important to remember that Aphrodite did have a little help. Although she was blessed with extraordinary beauty, she also wore a magic girdle that caused people to fall for her charms.

One of the myths of Aphrodite says she is the daughter of the god Zeus and the goddess of the oak tree, Dione. However, a more dramatic version of her birth involves the titan Cronos attacking his father Uranus, castrating him and throwing his sex organs into the sea, where they were tossed about in the foamy waves. The myth depicts Aphrodite being born from this, emerging out of the ocean and rising from within a great scallop shell.

Aphrodite was no stranger to romantic liaisons. She married the blacksmith Hephaestus, but then had an affair with his brother Ares, the god of war, and bore him three children. Aphrodite's greatest love, though, was Adonis. The myths say that when she saw Adonis as an infant she was so taken by his beauty that she hid him in a chest that she entrusted to Persephone, queen of the underworld.

Persephone was also captivated by Adonis – so much so that she refused to give him back. To settle the dispute, Zeus declared that Adonis was to spend part of the year in the underworld with Persephone and the rest of the time on earth with Aphrodite.

However, tragedy eventually struck – Adonis was mauled by wild beasts while hunting, and died in Aphrodite's arms. She sprinkled his blood where he lay, and from that place sprang the red anemone, a flower Aphrodite decreed to be short-lived, like her tragic love for Adonis.

 The god Hermes loved Aphrodite and they bore a child called Hermaphrodite

Aphrodite was graceful, creative and always had a lust for life

 Ancient pictures show Aphrodite riding a chariot drawn by swans

ARTEMIS

Artemis was known as the goddess of hunters and the queen of the wilderness. She roamed the mountains and woods and was often pictured with her bow and a quiver full of arrows. She asked Zeus for the gift of eternal virginity and was fiercely protective of her independence. Artemis ran wild and free in the world and encouraged a spirit of adventure and purity in her nymphs and followers.

She is also known as the protectress of childbirth – when she was born, her mother Leto suffered no labor pains. Artemis, who was immediately named goddess of the moon, then helped Leto as she struggled to deliver Artemis' twin, Apollo, who became god of the sun.

Artemis exuded confidence combined with strength and self-assuredness. She often told maidens, "You belong to yourself. No one man is your master." Together, she and her maidens hunted, yet protected, the animals of the forest, enjoying the thrill of the chase and the art of living in the wilderness.

Her nurturing spirit underpinned her intensely protective and private nature, and no man was ever allowed to see her naked. Once, though, when she was bathing in a stream, she noticed the hunter Actaeon spying on her. He was in the forest with his hounds, who were resting near the river. Artemis was so enraged that she turned Actaeon into a stag and incited his hounds to chase him and eventually tear him to pieces.

Artemis' beauty, strength and belief in her own values are inspirational even in modern times.

Artemis was born out of a liaison between Zeus and the nymph Leto

Along with Athena and Hestia, she was one of three virgin goddesses of Olympus

Artemis loved nature and cherished being able to roam free in the wilderness

HESTIA

Hestia was the goddess of the hearth and home and was calm, pure, and full of warmth. Synonymous with all things domestic, she also represented personal security and the importance of hospitality. If Martha Stewart were around in ancient Greece, she and Hestia would be swapping notes and exchanging decorating tips around the fireplace.

Ancient images of Hestia often depict her as a goddess who was comfortable with herself and didn't seek power, battle or victory in any of her relationships.

The fire of the hearth was often associated with Hestia; many consider this a symbol of the inner light which gives us vitality and energy in our lives. It's Hestia's warmth of spirit and genuine affection and hospitality that turn a house into a home.

Hestia's power came from quiet self-assurance, not from any blatant display of strength or assertiveness. She had a passion for home life and exuded elegance, grace and warmth.

 Hestia was one of the three virgin goddesses of Olympus

 Poseidon and Apollo wanted to marry her, but she refused

 She promised her brother Zeus that she would be a maiden forever

These gorgeous Greek goddesses were the role models of their time. They were a bunch of kick-ass female leaders who knew what they wanted and pursued their goals with passion and determination. And, for the most part, they did this while taking full advantage of the innate intuition that is nature's gift to every woman.

The good news is that you don't have to be a deity to harness your instincts and turn your dreams into reality. The ancient inspiration offered by these beautiful goddesses shows that identifying your passions and sticking to your key values is a firm foundation for success.

More importantly, you can draw on various aspects of these Greek goddesses' personalities to help you in different areas of life. Sometimes you might need Athena's tactical skill, or Demeter's determination, or Artemis' integrity. Their myths – combined with some practical, realistic strategies – can transform you into a gorgeous modern-day goddess. Before long, you'll be living a life that's divine, exciting, and truly magnificent.

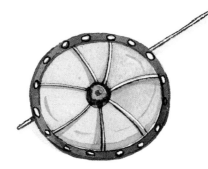

The Goddess in You

Are you a goddess?

A MODERN-DAY GODDESS IS A WOMAN WHO IS HAPPY, BEAUTIFUL, STRONG AND COMMITTED TO LIVING A LIFE OF PASSION AND EXCITEMENT. SHE BELIEVES IN HERSELF, IS TRUE TO HER VALUES. SHE KNOWS THAT HER DREAMS AND GOALS AREN'T LOFTY, DISTANT IDEALS — THE POWER TO MAKE THEM COME TRUE IS RIGHT IN HER HANDS.

This may sound like a really tall order; it might seem that today's goddesses are just as mythical as the ones from ancient Greece. Well let's get one thing straight before we go on. We're all goddesses. Simple as that. The trouble is, some of us are so busy living, working and playing that we end up suppressing our goddess nature, even though it is an inherent part of every woman.

Inside you is a gorgeous goddess, just waiting to shine. However, the reality is that there are probably times when you feel far from goddess-like! Whether you're having a bad hair day, are under a lot of stress at work or are just coping with a hectic schedule, it's not easy to feel fabulous in the midst of the stresses and challenges of modern-day living.

In between handling work commitments, fulfilling family obligations and keeping your social life buzzing, there's often very little time left for you. This means you're not giving your inner goddess much chance to flourish. But it's exactly these innate goddess instincts, talents and values that are going to help guide you successfully through life – you have this resource, full of untapped potential, within you.

Some women seem to connect with their inner goddess with ease – they appear confident, content and so together. It's as if they can breeze through life notching up personal and professional successes with little effort. Meanwhile, other women may find it tough just to get through the day.

To get onto the right path, all you have to do is nurture your natural gifts, trust your intuition, and give yourself permission to let your inner goddess shine.

Listening to your inner goddess

Your true goddess nature is something you're born with. It's more than just your genetic makeup: it's also your way of thinking, your innate gifts and your personal values. Listening to your inner goddess means paying attention to the things you genuinely feel are important to you.

This is why you need to identify your personal values – so you can make the distinction between what you think should be important and what truly matters. If you are aware of the principles or ethics that shape your life, you have a built-in benchmark or foundation you can lean on when faced with life's decisions.

But remember, other people's values may well be different from yours. Your attitudes and principles are molded by a variety of factors – parents, friends, school and spiritual or cultural influences – and for each of us, these factors operate a little (sometimes a lot) differently. Your core values are deeply personal, as are other people's, so be careful when you start comparing yours with theirs. The key is having a genuine respect for everyone else's way of thinking.

And when it comes to your own value system, the opinion that should matter most is yours – being able to stick by the values you consider important is vital if you want to lead a life you're happy with.

Artemis' integrity

Artemis, the goddess of hunters, valued her independence and was fiercely protective of her freedom. She trusted her intuition and was known for her integrity. Her followers knew she was committed to what she believed in.

Like Artemis, knowing and identifying your core values gives you an inner strength and peace. When you're faced with dilemmas – big or small – your values are the yardstick against which you measure your options.

For example, Belinda was offered a dream job opportunity at an advertising agency as a copywriter, complete with a great salary, lots of perks and huge career prospects. The job involved promoting cigarettes. Belinda was strongly opposed to smoking, particularly as her mother had suffered from a number of smoking-related illnesses.

Belinda said: "Despite what it could do for my career, I knew in my heart that the agency promoted something which was fundamentally at odds with my values. At first, I tried convincing myself that I could ignore it, and I almost accepted the job. But I knew I'd end up feeling guilty and resenting my employers." She didn't take the position.

If you feel something doesn't quite gel with your beliefs, listen to those warning bells. If, on the other hand, your options align with your core values, you'll find that you feel much more comfortable and secure in your decisions. Pay attention to your intuition. If you are feeling uneasy and that something's not quite right, it's your inner goddess trying to tell you something.

TURN YOUR DREAMS INTO REALITY

All goddesses love to dream. There's nothing more liberating than letting your imagination run wild and indulging in daydreams about exotic locales, exciting adventures, wonderful relationships, and fulfilling experiences.

However, goddesses also know that while having dreams and aspirations is fun, it's also important to turn them into concrete goals. And these goals can only be achieved if there is a practical plan backing them up. If you don't believe that your dreams can be transformed into reality, they will simply stay in the realm of your imagination.

So how do you go about making your dreams come true? It's one thing to believe it's possible, but it's another to create an achievable step-by-step plan of action. Let's work out what you actually need to do.

It may sound simple, but the first step is to figure out what your goals and dreams actually are. Many people know that they want their lives to be "better" or to "find a more fulfilling job," but few people can translate this into a definable goal. You may hear yourself saying things like, "I know I want a new job – but I don't know what I really want to do." Or perhaps you have a vague idea of what you want but don't have a clue about how to get there: "I'd love to travel the world but as it costs so much money and involves so much planning, I wouldn't know where to start."

Look at the different aspects of your life – your health, relationships, career, family, money, spirituality and hobbies – and think about the areas that don't seem to be working quite as well as you'd like.

Perhaps you'd like to improve your job prospects, or even change your career entirely, or maybe you'd like to maintain a healthy level of fitness and achieve an ideal weight. Perhaps you want to save for a down payment on a house, or perhaps your goal is something as simple as learning enough chords on the guitar so that you can play American Pie.

When you identify your goals and dreams, write them down. The simple act of putting these ideas down on paper helps you discover what you really want, and seeing your dreams on a "To Do" list moves them one step closer to reality.

So grab a notebook and your favorite milkshake or glass of red wine, let your imagination run free and think about what you really want out of life. You may even find your-self writing pages of things you'd love to do – after all, giving yourself permission to dream and achieve is liberating. So pick up your pen – and enjoy!

Dream big

Let yourself indulge in your wildest dreams and fantasies. Don't censor yourself; you may be tempted to not write down too many goals because you believe it's unrealistic to achieve all of them at once. While that may be true, you still need to give them a fighting chance.

Remember that your list of dreams or goals should involve both big and small aspirations. Don't be afraid of writing down something like, "Get a Ph.D. in physics" or "Launch my own line of clothing." These goals can sound so overwhelming and insurmountable you may think it's a waste of time to put them down at all. And you might even question if they are whimsical childhood fantasies or real desires of your heart. You'll soon find out – so make sure they're on the list.

Once you've compiled a decent list of goals and dreams, you need to work out the ones that really matter to you. Rank them in order of importance, or arrange them into groups with headings like "Would LOVE to achieve," "Would like to achieve if I have the time," and "Don't mind whether I achieve this or not."

Then concentrate on the ones you know you'd "love to achieve." If your goals aren't in this category, you probably won't have the drive or motivation to follow them through. That doesn't mean the goals that aren't in the top category won't see the light of day – you may be able to revisit those goals later, once you've already ticked off a few that are higher on your list of priorities.

Dream like a goddess

~ Allow yourself the freedom to dream. Write down anything you've always wanted to do, from smaller goals, such as joining the local gym, to more complex ones, such as getting an advanced degree. Look at everything, from your hobbies and interests to your career.

~ Think about any emotional or spiritual goals you may have. Perhaps you've always wanted to improve your relationship with your parents, or explore your religious faith. Write these goals down too.

~ Most importantly, allow yourself free rein to articulate your goals. Don't let yourself be limited by your current circumstances, skills, or financial position. In this exercise, indulge your inner desires – and dream big.

A PRACTICAL ACTION PLAN

Once you've identified the goals you want to pursue, you need to formulate a tangible plan of action to achieve them. Modern-day goddesses know that they have an innate power to make things happen, but like the goddesses of yesteryear, they also know how important it is to be grounded in reality.

Although writing down your goals and dreams may result in a whole list of items, you need to narrow this down to, say, the three goals that are most important to you. You can't tackle everything at once; if you spread yourself too thinly you won't be able to channel your attention effectively, and you will end up achieving very little.

Highlight the goals you want to concentrate on and deal with each of them individually. Once again, grab your notebook, write each goal on the top of a page and then write down all your thoughts about what you need to do to get you there. When you've done this, break down each idea even further, into smaller steps – the path to achieving your dreams needs to be divided into bite-sized steps.

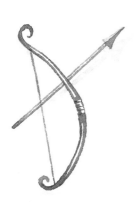

When you turn every one of these steps into a doable activity, and undertake to work through each one systematically, you're well on the way to making your dreams come true. It may sound too easy, but the reality is that it is that simple. The problem is that most people just don't bother doing it. Don't fall into this trap – work out your plan and start living the actions you need to get where you want to go.

PUT PROCRASTINATION IN ITS PLACE

The biggest obstacle to achieving your goals and dreams is not a lack of skill, finance or opportunity – it's procrastination. However, the good news is that this is within your control. Apart from making a commitment that you're going to pursue your goals and dreams, you also need to make sure you do what you can to make it easy to achieve what you want.

That's why figuring out doable activities is so important. A goal such as "renovate the spare room" becomes more doable when divided into smaller steps, such as:

~ Identify the furniture to keep or throw out
~ Donate unwanted furniture to a charity this weekend
~ Move the rest of the furniture into the hallway
~ Call the painter to make an appointment for a quote
~ Choose new colors from catalog or swatch book
~ Schedule the carpenter to build the shelves

The smaller the steps are, they easier they'll be to complete. You're less likely to put off something that's only going to take you a few minutes to do – like a simple phone call to the painter to schedule a time for him to visit. When you know that a task is achieveable, you're more likely to want to tackle it. And when you see yourself checking off items on your list of things to do, you'll be motivated to keep going.

Give yourself a fighting chance against procrastination by equipping yourself with a can-do attitude combined with a practical, step-by-step approach to achieving your goals. This isn't a magic formula that will make your dreams come true; it's a sensible, realistic way to accomplish what you want.

Sandra is a computer business analyst, but loves flowers. She wants to learn how to make creative floral arrangements and dreams of owning her own flower shop one day. This is how she broke down her big dream into little steps.

GOAL: TO LEARN FLORAL ART AND OPEN MY OWN FLOWER BUSINESS

Find out about floral art courses
- call local colleges to find out about part-time courses
- go to the library to find books on floristry
- ask local florists about the courses they recommend and research possibilities of any on-the-job training I can do on weekends

Research what's required to open a small business
- call government department to find out about required permits
- talk to other small business owners about their experiences
- read magazines and books on managing and running small businesses

Work out what money I need to do this
- make an appointment with my accountant
- do a cashflow analysis to determine exactly what my income and expenses are
- set aside a small amount of my salary each month to build up a nest-egg of capital

Explore possibilities of keeping my current job and working in floristry part-time
- find out how much vacation time and annual leave I have accrued
- ask about the possibility of working part-time next year
- offer my services to local florists if they need extra help during busy periods or for weekend weddings

Demeter's determination

When Demeter's daughter Persephone first disappeared, Demeter searched for her relentlessly. She roamed the world without eating or sleeping and was dedicated to her goal – being reunited with her daughter.

It's this single-minded determination that you can draw inspiration from. If your dream is close to your heart, your journey toward achieving it won't be a hard road; it will be a steady path that will eventually lead to results. Think of your dream as your "baby." If you nurture it with care and commitment, you're already halfway toward realizing your dream.

Career Goddesses

Transforming your work life

Let's face it. People spend most of their lives working, so it makes sense to try to work in a job that's enjoyable and fulfilling. When the bulk of your day is dedicated to your job, it's certainly a blessing if you can be passionate and excited about it. Imagine waking up each day knowing you're going to be paid for doing something you love.

Some cynics believe that any kind of work is destined to eventually turn into drudgery and boredom, and they don't believe it's possible for a job to generate enthusiasm or pleasure. If you have thoughts like this – or if you're surrounded by people who are trying to convince you that work is merely a necessary evil – stop, rewind, and think long and hard about whether you really want this to be your reality.

Modern-day goddesses know that work isn't just a series of jobs you do so the rent can be paid. Fulfilling careers can also be stimulating and inspiring, but to experience this you need to do the following things:

- figure out what your passions are
- combine this with your skills
- design a career you'll love

Some people may argue that for those with pressing financial responsibilities, a secure, steady job is much more practical than wide-eyed aspirations about dream jobs and soaring careers.

If money's a little tight, the idea of changing jobs – let alone careers – may be almost impossible to contemplate at the moment. But don't let yourself believe that it's not achievable when you haven't even tried yet. It's just that you may need to be a bit more creative than people who have fewer responsibilities or financial obligations in finding ways to make your dreams come true. Your decisions do need to be rooted in the real world, but you also need the fundamental belief that it can happen.

That's not to say there's some kind of mystical goddess formula that is going to transform your career – there isn't. Goddesses don't wave magic wands to realize their goals; they know that the only way to get anywhere is to work out a practical plan of action, using the techniques previously discussed.

Finding a job that inspires and motivates you is a priority for any career goddess. The problem is that many people aren't exactly sure what kind of job they should be looking for – they just know that their current one isn't fulfilling them. Basically, you'll enjoy your job a lot more if it involves work you're genuinely interested in, and if you're spending time on issues you're passionate about or working on projects you personally find exciting. To work out what your ideal job or career is, you first need to identify the best way to combine your existing skills with your personal passions.

This may mean considering a career change. If you've ended up with a career in sales, for instance, but can't stand dealing with customers and couldn't negotiate your way out of a paper bag, then it's safe to say you might be better suited to a different profession.

However, a radical career change isn't always the answer. Sometimes all you need to do is tweak your current job so that it becomes more fulfilling and rewarding.

Katrina, for example, was an accountant for a clothing manufacturer, but she was unfulfilled at her job and dreamt of working in the entertainment industry. Katrina said: "I was so bored, but when I really thought about my skills and interests, I realized that I actually enjoyed using my accounting skills. I just wasn't at all inspired by the manufacturing industry or the company I worked for.

"I figured that if I wanted to get into the world of showbiz, one way was to take advantage of my current skills as a way in. I contacted every movie studio, production house and entertainment-related company I could find in this city and actually ended up with three job interviews. Now I'm working in the finance department of a small movie distributor and I love it."

So how do you figure out what your dream job might be?

~ Write a list of all your skills. Include everything from your professional skills and technical expertise to personal skills such as cooking or playing the piano.

~ List your main interests and passions. It doesn't matter whether you love sports, fashion, technology or art, just identify the areas you're most excited about.

~ Brainstorm ideas on how you can combine your skills with your interests. Write down everything you can think of – even ideas that seem ludicrous – then see if anything you've written captures your imagination.

For example, Samantha was a public relations coordinator who also loved fashion, drawing and collecting vintage handbags. Two years ago, she worked out her dream job possibilities …

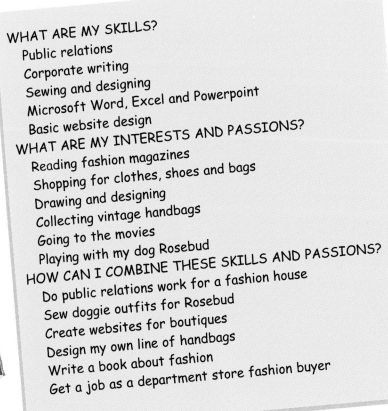

WHAT ARE MY SKILLS?
  Public relations
  Corporate writing
  Sewing and designing
  Microsoft Word, Excel and Powerpoint
  Basic website design
WHAT ARE MY INTERESTS AND PASSIONS?
  Reading fashion magazines
  Shopping for clothes, shoes and bags
  Drawing and designing
  Collecting vintage handbags
  Going to the movies
  Playing with my dog Rosebud
HOW CAN I COMBINE THESE SKILLS AND PASSIONS?
  Do public relations work for a fashion house
  Sew doggie outfits for Rosebud
  Create websites for boutiques
  Design my own line of handbags
  Write a book about fashion
  Get a job as a department store fashion buyer

When Samantha thought about this list, the idea that appealed to her most was having her own label and designing handbags. However, transforming herself from a public relations coordinator into a successful handbag designer didn't happen overnight – it required determination, patience and a firm commitment to taking action.

Samantha committed herself to the goal of creating her own label and started designing and sewing bags in her spare time. When friends began admiring and ordering from her, she gained more confidence that her designs could appeal to a wider market.

"I designed and made bags on most weekends, and eventually I realized that my hobby could be a real business. I was so excited about it, but I knew I had to spend more time on it if I wanted to get anywhere. It took months of negotiation, but I managed to persuade my boss to let me work three days a week. It was a bit of a gamble, because my bags could have flopped.

"I worked out a plan for how to organize my time, find the right suppliers, sell to retail outlets and deal with my finances. I used my PR skills to get publicity for my label. Working part-time gave me the chance to launch my first line. Then, after six months, I finally quit my public relations job to concentrate on my new career as a handbag designer!"

Apart from combining her skills and passions, the key to Samantha successfully creating her dream job was that she developed a concrete, step-by-step strategy to get her there. To achieve your own career goal, break down what you have to do into small steps, and create your very own action plan.

GETTING AHEAD GODDESS-STYLE

If you want to succeed in style, there are a few things you can do to give yourself an extra edge. Career goddesses know that it takes more than skills and qualifications to make things happen; you also need the right attitude, great people skills and confidence in your ability.

A creative environment

The environment you work in can have a huge impact on your effectiveness. While some people may have a comfortable physical space to work in, not everyone is blessed with a fabulous job environment. If that's the case for you, you can still do things to make your workplace better – not only will it affect your productivity, it'll simply be a nicer place to be!

If there's one fundamental rule all career goddesses should follow it's to aim to have an uncluttered workspace. A desk or workspace that's piled with papers and cluttered with materials is going to be harder to work around, and will cause a certain level of stress – and that's added pressure that can be easily eliminated. Keep your documents filed, your coffee cup washed and your papers arranged in order of priority. Some projects do  require a degree of organized chaos, it's true, but you'll know the difference – if your work environment could do with a makeover, haul out the trash can and do some spring cleaning.

Personalize your workspace
Once you've de-cluttered, add a few touches to give your workspace that extra something. We don't mean you need to renovate the department or overhaul your work station; just do things that will make your workspace feel familiar and comfortable. This isn't a suggestion for sticking up a wall full of photos of friends and family; one or two photos are okay, but don't go overboard. But if simple things – like getting a more comfortable chair, changing your screen saver, or simply using a new mousepad – will make a difference, do them. It doesn't take much effort, and if it helps create a more enjoyable work environment, it's worth it.

Know your worth at work

Let's say you've been working hard for the past year. Your efforts have made a difference and you feel it's time for a raise even though your boss hasn't scheduled your performance review yet. How do you get paid what you're worth without having to beg for or demand more money?

The first thing not to do is march into your boss' office and start banging the table, complaining that the long hours you're putting in aren't worth the pittance you receive in your pay check. That's not going to win you any points.

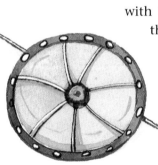

However, it is important to speak formally with your boss or supervisor about these things. You might think your boss must know you've made a huge effort and gone above and beyond the call of duty, but this could be a misguided assumption. While some bosses are clued up on who the good performers on their team are, others may simply be too busy to notice. This is where you need to blow your own trumpet a little and make your achievements clearly known.

If you want a pay rise, you need to convince them you're worth it. This means selling yourself, almost as if you're in a job interview. Show them how you've contributed to projects, being as specific as you can. For example, instead of saying "I worked until 9:00 p.m. every night last month," turn that into a statement where they can understand the results: "I worked late every night last month so that we could meet the deadline on the sales pitch. And it was worth the effort – we got the job."

Once you have your boss's attention, it's time to negotiate your raise. To work out how much you should be paid, check job ads, inquire with recruitment agencies and figure out a salary level that you're comfortable and happy with. If your boss comes back with a lower figure than you expected, keep negotiating. If you don't feel you're being paid what you're worth, you won't put in as much effort or you could end up resenting your job.

Are you in the money?

If you think you deserve a raise at work:
~ Check out job ads and find out the salary range for similar
jobs in your industry
~ Don't compare your salary to your colleagues' if
you're not meant to know what they're earning
~ Compile a list of achievements or successful projects where
you've been an integral member of the team
~ Outline the duties you undertake even though they might
not be part of your job description
~ Identify any extra courses or training you've done to show
you're serious about learning new skills and advancing your career
~ make an appointment with your boss to discuss your career path
~ List the reasons why you think you deserve a raise
~ Be prepared that you may not get an answer immediately
~ Listen to feedback your boss may have

Building relationships

Developing relationships in the workplace is vital if you want to get any-where – you can't expect to work in isolation. And even if you're skilled and competent, that's not going to make a difference if no one knows what you're capable of.

Some ambitious types know what they want to achieve and will do any-thing they can to get there, regardless of who they have to step on to accom-plish this. However, career goddesses know that true success comes from having a genuine connection with colleagues and supervisors alike.

However, some go-getters misinterpret this, and believe it means making friends or forming strategic alliances with the company's movers and shakers. This transparent approach isn't going to win you any friends and is a short-sighted tactic that's potentially destructive.

Genuine respect

Successful goddesses, those who have the respect of their peers and bosses, have developed genuine relationships with co-workers. They don't just nurture alliances with the colleagues or managers they think will be the most useful to their careers. Even if you were to try this approach, which is pretty manipulative, it would likely fail, because perceptions of who the most influential people are in your office can be skewed, and the most unexpected person could end up being the next head of your department. People who call their allies too early are often in for a fall.

Ultimately, it's simply far more satisfying to know you have genuine relationships with your co-workers and superiors. Apart from the fact that you'll know you're acting with integrity, you'll develop a reputation your colleagues will respect.

Athena's action

Athena, the warrior queen, was resourceful, savvy and determined. While we're not suggesting you go to war in your workplace, Athena's courage and strength can provide inspiration when the demands of your career are overwhelming.

Rather than allowing work pressures to get on top of you, try to develop a "take charge" approach and tackle the challenges of your job by using a sensible, systematic plan. Use Athena's method for working out a strategy for battle: think of the big picture first, then specify the finer details. Write down your ultimate goals and the steps you need to take to get there.

Draw on your inner strength to confront what lies ahead. As you begin to achieve the small steps, you'll find yourself gaining more confidence — and motivation — to tackle other issues. Before long, you'll find, as Athena did, that what looked like impossible tasks are just challenges.

Goddesses in Love

THE POWER OF ONE

THE ANCIENT GODDESSES CHAMPIONED INDEPENDENCE, FREEDOM, AND A HEALTHY SENSE OF SELF-WORTH. IT'S NOT THAT THEY DIDN'T CHERISH LOVE AND RELATIONSHIPS, IT'S JUST THAT THEY KNEW THE IMPORTANCE OF NURTURING THEIR OWN SELF-ESTEEM AND FEEDING THEIR PERSONAL NEEDS AND INTERESTS BEFORE ATTEMPTING TO SHARE THEIR LIVES WITH SOMEONE ELSE.

Relationships take time, energy, and emotional investment. Before you can truly develop a healthy love relationship, you need to be comfortable in your own skin, happy with where your life is heading, and aware of your emotional and spiritual needs. It may be a cliché, but it's true: you have to be happy within yourself before you can be happy with anyone else.

So it's vital to embrace being alone. Yes, that's right. Being single is a blessing – apart from being an integral part of self-discovery, it can also be a hell of a lot of fun.

Society or family expectations often put pressure on women to partner with a man. We end up believing that unless we're in a relationship, there's something wrong. And Hollywood movies that depict hearts, flowers and lots of soft focus happily-ever-after scenes make single women wonder if they're missing out.

However, modern-day goddesses know this is a trap – fairytale endings simply don't happen unless we're ready for them. And this means being comfortable about being single. Think about it. Who do you think is more attractive? A confident, sociable woman glowing with positivity or a woman who is worried about finding a man because she's desperate to be in a relationship?

Modern-day goddesses know that it's important to make the most of being a sassy, savvy single – and that there is a lot you can do now that isn't so easy when you're in a relationship. This is a time when you can broaden your horizons, meet new people and travel to exotic places. If you are free of the responsibilities of a relationship, it's a great opportunity to take risks and pursue your passions.

Demeter's nurturing spirit

Just as Demeter presided over harvesting and the earth's abundance, modern-day goddesses like you need to develop a nurturing and caring spirit – especially when it comes to you. To be able to reap real benefits – in love or in any aspect of life – you need to invest time in your own self-development and happiness.

If you find yourself saying things like: "I'd love to go to Paris, but it's such a romantic place, I'd rather wait till I'm in a relationship," or "I want go to design school but it would be so much easier if I had a partner to support me," stop this kind of talk! Thinking this way is dangerous. Your personal desires shouldn't hinge on whether or not you're in relationship. Invest in yourself and the rewards will follow.

THE RULES OF ATTRACTION

So what is it that makes some women seem so attractive? These modern goddesses relate to other people with ease and have an indefinable charisma that seems to draw people to them. It's easy to think they must have the modern equivalent of Aphrodite's magic girdle. However, the reality is that there's no magic involved at all.

The fundamental rule of attraction comes down to a healthy self-image. This is what underpins how attractive others perceive us to be. Remember, before you can have a truly successful partnership with someone else, you need to be happy being on your own. And if you truly embrace life as a single person and are comfortable with who you are, you'll exude a warmth and confidence that are not only attractive, they're infectious. People want to be around people who have a positive outlook on life; we're all naturally drawn to people who make us feel good.

So when you've reached the stage where you're confident and happy about not being in a relationship, don't be surprised if your attractiveness quotient suddenly goes through the roof.

Aphrodite's charm

As goddess of beauty and love, Aphrodite had bucketloads of charisma – and she knew it! She had a confidence and poise that amazed people all over the world; they were in awe of her beauty and charm. Modern-day Aphrodites have the same kind of attractive spirit – but they're just regular girls with a great attitude and a healthy body image.

GORGEOUS AND GLAMOROUS. Ask yourself: "Am I too dressed up?" Then say: "Who cares?" Don't be worried if you look too gorgeous! Why bother wondering if you look "normal' or "down-to-earth" enough – if you're looking stunning, why tone it down? Sure, it pays to use common sense, and you don't want to turn up in a ball gown when you're going to a barbecue at the beach, but in the normal course of work or socializing, don't repress your inner beauty – give yourself permission to shine!

LOOK AFTER YOURSELF. A good body image doesn't just appear overnight. It needs to be cultivated – give yourself positive affirmations that you're a beautiful, worthwhile goddess, and back them up with concrete actions to validate this attitude. Do whatever it is that makes you feel gorgeous, whether it's sticking to a fitness plan or indulging in regular facials or massages – or both! Think of it all as an investment in your self-esteem.

Routine versus romance

Goddesses know that partnerships need love and attention if they're going to succeed. Whether you're in a long-term partnership or still in the honeymoon period of dating, your relationship can benefit from a little extra sparkle. Sometimes we are so comfortable with our partners that we forget how magical romance can be. It may be cozy and familiar to rent a DVD, cook at home and snuggle together on the sofa, but if this has been your Saturday night activity for the past six months, perhaps it's time to think about revitalizing your relationship routine.

Stephanie and Marco, for example, have been together for over three years. Although they both enjoy the comforts of domestic bliss, they still continue to surprise each other – literally. Once a month one of them plans a mystery date (they alternate months), so each month one of them is completely surprised by what's in store. It's something they did when they first started dating, and both of them loved the mystery so much that they're still doing it, still surprising each other on their monthly dates. Their outings have ranged from a simple gourmet picnic in the park to an elaborate affair involving a sailing boat, a beautiful dinner, and stargazing at the local observatory.

Dates don't have to be complex or fancy – if you put in a little bit of effort and plan them from the heart, you'll weave a magical memory that will be cherished for years to come.

Let's say you are in a relationship. On one hand, there's the heady intoxication of love and infatuation. Your heart beats faster, the sun shines brighter and, for a while, the world looks like a Hollywood movie, complete with a schmaltzy ending. Sometimes, life really does live up to the fairytale.

However, on the other hand, being in the real world means there are no guarantees for a happy and successful relationship. There is one thing that will get you halfway there, though: communication. It sounds like such a simple thing, but many people fail to communicate effectively with their partners.

By this we don't just mean the simple art of talking – anyone can chat about their favorite football team or television show. The first step toward real communication with your partner is to develop a way to comfortably share your feelings with each other. We're not talking about mushy "I love you" statements – that's the easy part!

The challenge is being able to talk through issues or problems. Sometimes, when you're confronted with a difficult situation, your first reaction is to avoid dealing with it. As a result, it gets swept under the carpet – but it's guaranteed to resurface later, by which time it may be a time bomb ready to explode. Often these "bombs" could have been defused much earlier if you bothered to talk about them.

The trouble is that we often assume too much – we think we know what our partner is thinking or feeling. So instead of basing decisions on perceptions that may be way off base, make a commitment to each other to truly share your thoughts and feelings. Lay aside any judgments, encourage honesty – and simply communicate.

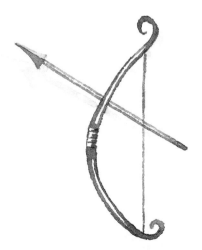

KISSING FROGS

Even goddesses kiss their fair share of frogs before finding a relationship that seems right. But encountering men who are wrong for you isn't a bad thing – it's a normal part of life. And unless you intend to live in a cocoon, it's inevitable. Not recognizing that they're bad for you is what makes things complicated.

Who you meet in life is a bit of a gamble, but goddesses are savvy women who know that playing the game of love involves a lot of fun, a touch of adventure and perhaps a little bit of heartache. Like any good gambler, the key to tilting the balance in the right direction, in terms of the men you've been dealt, is to know when to hold them and when to fold them.

Paying attention to warning bells that scream "Frog alert" is another way to keep the odds in your favor. Here are some of those warning bells:

"I'm not looking for a serious relationship." Some women hear these words and still plunge headfirst into a romance, hoping that he'll change his mind once he's had a chance to experience their love. Put simply, if he's bothered to tell you that he doesn't want a serious relationship, don't expect anything different.

"I need some space." Admittedly, we all need time alone to chill out and be by ourselves. So, in the first instance, give him the benefit of the doubt – he may genuinely need some time for himself. But if he's using this line on a regular basis and you feel like a second-choice filler date, then either suggest that he prioritizes you back into his life or stop and think about whether or not you want to spend time with someone who writes you in pencil in his daybook.

"I'm bringing over my laundry." Domestic bliss and being comfortable enough to share in the day-to-day chores in life is one thing. But if you find yourself doing the sorts of things his mother used to do, think again. If you simply love doting on him, that's okay, but if he expects you to pick up after him, do his laundry or make his lunch, give him some bus money and draw him a map out of your life! You don't want a kid, you want a partner.

"Let me explain. It's not what you think." While it's wise to give your guy the benefit of the doubt if you find him in a compromising situation, it's also important not to kid yourself. There comes a time when you need to be brutally honest about your relationship. The trouble is, women tend to be forgiving creatures. And sometimes you may overlook his transgressions if he oozes enough charm and puts on that innocent it-wasn't-me look. If he tells you he's working late, but comes home with whisky on his breath and lipstick on his collar, tell him to leapfrog out of your life.

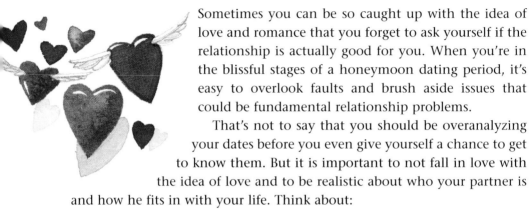

Sometimes you can be so caught up with the idea of love and romance that you forget to ask yourself if the relationship is actually good for you. When you're in the blissful stages of a honeymoon dating period, it's easy to overlook faults and brush aside issues that could be fundamental relationship problems.

That's not to say that you should be overanalyzing your dates before you even give yourself a chance to get to know them. But it is important to not fall in love with the idea of love and to be realistic about who your partner is and how he fits in with your life. Think about:

Compatibility. Quite simply, do you get along? Does conversation flow and do you laugh at the same things – or do you find yourself struggling to come up with things to talk about? A basic capacity to relate to each other is vital. It may sound obvious, but some people are so relieved to finally be in a relationship that they forget to focus on whether their partner is actually right for them.

The basics. Are there any fundamental differences that mean your relationship's long-term success is in jeopardy? Fairytales might have you believing that "love will conquer all," but if your partner has values which are at odds to yours – perhaps the two of you are strongly committed to different faiths or one of you wants children, but the other is dead against it – you need to ask yourself if it's worth the pain that's sure to follow.

Expectations. This is where communication is vital: you need to find out if you're both on the same page. Are you aware of each other's expectations of the relationship? Sure, if you're still in the early stages of dating, it's probably premature to talk about the future, but ultimately you need to establish what you both want – whether it's a casual dating experience or something more long-term.

Handling conflict. Any couple that says they never argue is lying. Disagreements are inevitable, so instead of dreading or avoiding them, accept that they're part of the normal course of a relationship and commit to resolving them. Remember that a head-in-the-sand   approach doesn't mean the problem will go away; it won't. Resolving conflicts may not be easy, and you both may end up having to compromise, but no relationship can survive if problems are regularly left to simmer until they boil over.

The Domestic Goddess

TREAT YOURSELF LIKE A GODDESS

BEING A DOMESTIC GODDESS DOES NOT MEAN YOU'RE A WHIZ IN A KITCHEN OR SKILLED AT HANDICRAFTS. IT'S ALL ABOUT NURTURING YOURSELF ENOUGH TO FEEL EMPOWERED AND VITALIZED. TAKING TIME OUT FOR YOURSELF IS AN ESSENTIAL PART OF BEING A GORGEOUS GODDESS.

In your hectic life, you might feel as if you're always rushing – from a client meeting to a seminar, then to an aerobics class, then to drinks with friends. Even though you might enjoy, and perhaps even thrive on, this busy timetable, it's still crucial that you schedule blocks of "Me Time" in your diary.

This is time when all you need to worry about is you, when you can be alone, with nothing but your thoughts for company. It's the only way you'll be able to clear your mind of the pressures of work and life and find out what your body wants and what your emotional and spiritual needs are.

Block off some time for yourself, and make sure you don't cheat by filling it in with going to the movies or reading the latest best-selling novel. This means you're still occupying your mind and keeping yourself entertained. You're not giving yourself a chance to experience the ultimate goddess treatment – time when you really get to nurture your soul and listen to your inner desires.

Attitude versus activity

You may understand the importance of relaxation and downtime on an intellectual level, but it's also vital to put it into practice. Don't get confused – relaxation doesn't mean a long session on the treadmill in the gym or a skiing holiday. Relaxation is about having the right attitude, not doing the right activity.

Let's take the example of the working up a sweat on the treadmill. You may think that you find a heavy-duty workout like this relaxing, but if you are the kind of person who thrives on adrenaline and pressure at work, you will only think it's relaxing because you're throwing your body into yet another situation that involves pressure and produces adrenaline. Remember, enjoyment is not the same as relaxation.

There's nothing wrong with going to the gym or playing sports, but they are goal-oriented activities – perhaps you want to lift heavier weights or win at tennis – rather than relaxation activities.

Whatever you choose as a form of relaxation will only work if it helps you spend quality time with yourself.

Time for reflection

Nurture your inner goddess by doing something that's enjoyable and fun, but also gives you time for reflection. Here are some ideas:

~ Book yourself in for a massage, facial or some kind of pampering. You'll be giving your body a therapeutic, revitalizing treatment and your mind a chance to bliss out and relax. Even though it's fun to have pampering days like this with your girlfriends, avoid the mid-manicure gossip session and treat yourself to an afternoon of solitude.

~ Do some gentle exercise where you can enjoy fresh air, get your circulation going, and simply appreciate the great outdoors. Don't be tempted to go for a strenuous run or do a cardio class – you'll be pounding your body and concentrating on achieving some kind of physical goal. Instead, pick an easy exercise activity that will clear the cobwebs from your mind but still give you a chance for reflection.

~ Find your favorite spot – perhaps by the beach, a scenic picnic area, or your local park – and simply sit there and watch life go by. Don't bring a book or a Discman. Think of this as a quiet time where you can de-clutter your mind of life's distractions and let your real feelings come to the forefront. If you have a hectic schedule you might think this time could be better spent catching up on chores or taking your car to the mechanic. In fact, blocking in your diary "Me Time" is just as important as those other activities.

~ Keep a diary. It's useful to be able to put your thoughts down on paper and meditate on what you've written. Put your pen to paper and simply let your feelings flow – the only person who is going to read it is you. Or perhaps keep a "thanks" diary, listing the things you're thankful for, whether it's a job promotion or something as simple as a beautiful sunny day. It's a great way to stay positive and appreciate the little things in life.

~ Before you go to bed, clear your mind and give yourself the best possible chance for a restful sleep. Again, even though it's tempting to read before bed, this means you're keeping your mind active right up until you turn out the light. Instead, put on some soothing music, concentrate on your breathing and let your thoughts simply drift for about 20 minutes.

SENSE AND SENSUALITY

Stimulating and awakening your senses – whether it's by listening to your favorite music, indulging in hokey-pokey ice cream or sleeping on crisp, cotton sheets – is an essential part of appreciating life. Indulging your sense of smell, sight, taste, sound, and touch means you can turn simple experiences into little luxuries.

Celebrating your sensuality is also important – modern-day goddesses are all sensual beings, and it's healthy to be aware of what gives you pleasure. We're not necessarily talking about sex here – it's not about buying sexy lingerie and organizing a romantic rendezvous with your lover. Exploring your sensuality is something that can be done with or without a partner.

It can be as simple as filling your bathtub, adding essential oils and sprinkling in some rose petals. Let the flowers brush your skin, inhale the beautiful scent and feel the warmth and coziness of the water. Or how about wearing beautiful silk underwear underneath your work clothes – even if the

only person who is going to see it is you! Some people may think this is a waste of time, but it'll feel great against your skin, and knowing that you look great, both on the surface and under your layers, will give you a boost throughout the day. Don't feel guilty about nurturing your sensuality; think of it as an essential part of revitalizing your senses and making you feel alive.

CREATING A HEAVENLY HOME

Living in a home that's fit for a goddess is a simple pleasure that all women can experience. This doesn't mean you need expensive furnishings; you just need to find somewhere that suits your needs and personality. Your home is a place where you should feel safe and welcome, a place where you can chill out and feel free to be completely yourself.

Many magazines are full of unrealistic pictures of stylish homes that can make us feel that ours are very ordinary. But, as the saying goes, your home is your castle – not anyone else's. So it's important to develop surroundings where you can be comfy, content, and calm.

Perhaps you don't have your own home yet. Maybe you're living with family or sharing with friends and you're not in a position to transform the whole house or apartment. You can still apply the same principles to your bedroom, though, or to whichever area is your domain. As a modern-day goddess, you need a special place that is yours alone.

Hestia's home

As goddess of hearth and home, Hestia knew the vital role that a home played in people's lives. In ancient times, the hearth was a central part of domestic life – used for cooking and for generating warmth. It was always looked after and kept alight. You can draw inspiration from Hestia and create a home that soothes your soul and rekindles your energy. Here are a few guidelines for creating your own goddess sanctuary:

~ Make it personal – hang up your favorite pictures, display precious mementos, stick photos on the fridge and surround yourself with things that make your home special to you.

~ Let go of the past – is there anything in your home that evokes unpleasant memories, or a bit of furniture that you simply don't like? Get rid of it. Sell it, give it away or throw it in the trash.

~ Color your senses – paint the walls in colors that suit the room. For example, soothing colors like pastels and light blues or greens are suitable for rooms where you want to chill out and relax.

~ Turn simple into special – you don't need fancy décor items in your home. Little things like candles, aromatherapy burners, beautiful soaps, and a simple bunch of fresh flowers can add luxury without costing a fortune.

SWEEP AWAY LIFE'S CLUTTER

There's nothing more liberating than de-cluttering your home. This is a chance to throw out boxes of junk, clear your cupboard space, and free your wardrobe of last decade's fashion mistakes. Apart from being a very practical exercise, it can also be an emotionally cleansing experience.

We attach many memories and emotions to things, objects, and mementos. While you need to keep hold of precious souvenirs and keepsakes, it's also important to clear away things which may be cluttering your life or keeping you from moving on. Goddesses should perform a regular de-cluttering ritual – think of it as spring cleaning your home and your life at the same time.

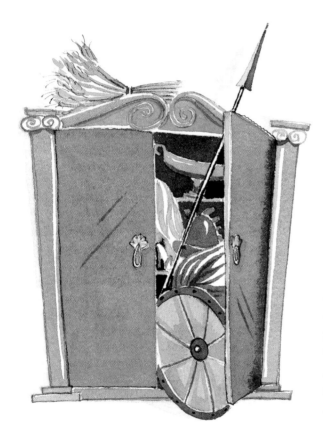

Wardrobe wars. Promise yourself you'll be ruthless, then fling open your closet doors and purge your shelves and hangers of anything you haven't worn in 18 months. It may be hard getting rid of your old prom dress or the Madonna-inspired pointy-bra outfit that hasn't seen the light of day for years, but it has be done. Try to consider it not as a painful separation from your favorite old clothes, but as a liberating experience – an opportunity to clear out your old "selves" to make room for new ones. But don't just throw the clothes in the trash – have a garage sale, donate your clothes to charity or give them away to friends.

Fix it. Like most people, you probably have many things that need small repairs. The trouble with minor repairs – like buttons that have fallen off or lightbulbs that need replacing – is that we never get around to fixing them.

We'll fix a hole in the roof or a noisy muffler well before we pay attention to a wobbly table leg that merely needs a dab of superglue. Write a list of things that need fixing, set aside an afternoon to tackle them, and check them off as you go. You'll be amazed at your sense of achievement when you get it all done.

Clutter-free living. Go through your whole home – or your room, if you haven't got your own pad yet – and do a "clutter audit." Are there any areas which need a mini spring cleaning? Approach these areas with the same ruthlessness with which you attacked your clothes. If you have a drawer full of nail polishes, but only ever use the same three colors, get rid of the rest. Or maybe you have piles of magazines you've been meaning to read, or cupboards full of knickknacks you don't particularly like, but have kept over the years simply because it hasn't occurred to you to throw them out. Grab a box and de-clutter. Be brutal.

Bedroom bliss. Pay special attention to your bedroom. If there's one area that needs to be free from clutter, it's the place where you sleep. If your bedroom is full of mess and confusion, that's the last image you'll see before going to bed, and even if you block out the untidiness, you'll still subconsciously know that you're lying in the midst of chaos. If your bedroom is a peaceful, uncluttered environment, you're more likely to have a tranquil sleep.

Be a Gorgeous Goddess

HEALTH AND VITALITY

THE FUNDAMENTAL FACTOR IN BEING A GORGEOUS GODDESS IS TO GLOW WITH HEALTH AND VITALITY. THIS MEANS TREATING YOUR BODY WITH THE RESPECT IT DESERVES. IT'S NOT ABOUT WEIGHT OR SPORTING PROWESS – IT'S ABOUT MAINTAINING A HEALTHY LIFESTYLE AND LISTENING TO WHAT YOUR BODY NEEDS.

Keeping your body in tune is the first step to fostering a healthy mind and spirit. If you aren't functioning well physically, it impacts on everything else in your life. Putting your body under pressure from illness or stress affects everything, from your productivity at work to your emotional health.

Looking after your body is about paying attention to two basic areas – nutrition and fitness. Ask yourself: am I eating a balanced diet and do I get enough exercise? If your answers to both are no, don't panic – it doesn't mean you have to suddenly become a vegetarian or begin training for the Boston marathon.

When it comes to nourishment, our bodies expect a wide variety of food – and yes, that includes dessert! The key principle is to consume the foods you enjoy, but in moderation.

With exercise, don't subject yourself to a fitness regime you hate. It just doesn't make sense. Many people have the misconception that all exercise is boring or painful. That is simply not true. Find an activity that's interesting and enjoyable – you're much more likely to stick to an exercise or sport if you're having fun!

FIT FOR LIVING

If you already lead a fairly active life, all you need to do is make a commitment to maintaining your level of exercise. However, to ensure that your fitness regime doesn't become boring, think about trying out new sports – apart from learning extra skills and meeting new people, you may discover a whole new passion.

If you haven't been very proactive in the area of exercise and want to look at ways you can improve your fitness, you need to create a simple plan that you know you can stick to. Having a vague idea that you might want to do more exercise is unlikely to translate into real action until you are more specific about what you plan to do.

Changing your lifestyle

Julie-Anne made a New Year's resolution to become fit and healthy. Her goal: "Improve my fitness and do more exercise." However, this statement was way too broad; it needed to be broken down into smaller, more defined steps. Julie-Anne realized she had to write down doable tasks that would help her achieve her goal. For example, specific tasks such as "Go for a 30-minute walk three times a week" and "Book a fitness assessment at the gym" are clearer and more manageable.

Be realistic about the changes you want to make to your lifestyle and begin incorporating them slowly. Ultimately, you want your healthy new habits to integrate seamlessly into your life, so start with small changes and stick to them until they become a normal part of your life.

If you hardly ever exercise, going for a 30-minute walk three times a week will be quite a change to your regular routine. Even though your body may cope with it okay, you simply won't be used to exercising so frequently. If it's too much of a shock to your lifestyle, you won't stick to it. Start off by exercising once a week for a couple of weeks, and gradually build up to three times a week. Ease yourself into it and commit to your plan until your new activity becomes second nature.

BEING BEAUTIFUL

It goes without saying that goddesses are beautiful. They also know that an essential part of looking good is feeling great. When you like the way you look, there will be valuable flow-on effects – improved self-esteem and confidence. So it makes sense to invest time in whatever it takes to make you feel like the goddess you truly are.

Being beautiful doesn't involve spending hours in front of the mirror or buying the latest fashions. And it's certainly not about primping and preening in order to be attractive to men. The only person you should be wanting to impress is yourself.

Figure out what you can do to make yourself feel great. Perhaps it's something as simple as a facial or a spritz of perfume. Or maybe you'll feel like a goddess if you're wearing just the right pair of Manolo Blahnik shoes. The amount of effort you put into making yourself feel beautiful will depend on your needs and your personality.

Some women want the works – nails done, hair styled, and outfits put together just so – whereas other women may be happy with a simple dab of lip gloss. Both these scenarios, and everything in between, are perfectly valid. If it's going to make you feel good about yourself, it's worth it.

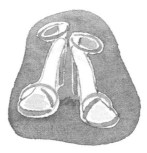

Persephone's paradox

Persephone represented two very different worlds – darkness and light. But she moved naturally between the two during different parts of the year. She was able to transform herself in order to thrive in whatever environment she was faced with.

Life is full of ups and downs, and one of the ways of coping when you're dealt a few blows is to draw on Persephone's inspiration. Believe that you will inevitably come out of the darkness – it's just a matter of time.

As a modern-day goddess you need to realize that the power to adapt and change your reality is in your hands. Sometimes you may feel fairly low, even downright depressed. However, you have a choice: you can accept this as the way it is or be proactive and try to improve the way you feel.

Actively doing things that make you feel better is essential if you want to move from one headspace to another. Whether or not you consciously think about it, the very fact that you're being proactive means you have a practical plan to help you move from darkness to light. It also represents the fact that you have hope for the future – and recognizing and embracing that can make all the difference.

WHAT YOUR IMAGE SAYS ABOUT YOU

Have you ever thought about what kind of image you're projecting to others and if their perception of you reflects reality? The way other people see you influences the way they treat you.

If your body language and demeanor say, "Don't bother looking at me, I'm not that important," that's exactly how you'll be treated. However, if your attitude says, "I'm a gorgeous goddess, I deserve respect and dignity," then you'll find yourself commanding precisely that kind of response.

Modern-day goddesses know that conveying a positive image is important. You need to appear approachable and warm, yet confident and assertive. Think about the following:

Make eye contact: Look people in the eye when you talk to them. Avoiding eye contact makes you look nervous, or preoccupied or not particularly interested in what the person you're talking to has to say. Maintaining eye contact will help the people around you feel at ease and give you a warm, welcoming demeanor.

Walk tall: The way you hold yourself says a lot about your attitude. Walking confidently, sporting a friendly smile, with your head held high, will score you a lot more points than if you're slouching around, shuffling your feet and looking unsure whether you're coming or going.

Treat others with respect: Don't expect to be treated well if you're not prepared to do the same in return. It's fruitless being selective about who should get your respect; the reality is that all human beings deserve it. Be generous in esteeming other people and you will reap the benefits.

An Abundant Life

Modern-day goddesses know that life is full of wonderful blessings and rich experiences. Sure, it also serves up a few rough patches along the way, but on the whole, life's abundance is within our grasp.

When some people think about living an abundant life they focus on money. However, goddesses know that how much cash they have in the bank is not the issue. Living a life that's rich and varied goes way beyond mere financial figures. It's about creating opportunities, valuing your blessings and being lucky enough to go through some pretty special experiences along the way.

THE MYTH OF MONEY

Aiming to accumulate as much wealth as you can is a very narrow view. It's natural to aim for financial security, and there's certainly nothing wrong with making money, but don't let the pursuit of wealth overshadow other important aspects of life.

Instead, work on being in control of your finances – knowing where your money is going and how it's working for you means you're in a better position to make informed decisions that will impact your life.

• STEP 1: BUDGET BASICS. It's simple to work out your budget. (most advisers would tell you to do the budget first: work out your expenses, including money for entertainment and clothes etc, and compare it with your income, then see what you can afford to put away as savings each week.) First, write down your weekly income, then add up your typical expenses over a week, dividing your expenses into different categories, such as rent, entertainment, food, gas, utilities, transportation, charitable donations and other items (some of these items might come as quarterly or annual payments: do the math to work out what they are as a weekly expense). Then factor in extra costs for possible one-time expenses – such as a vacation or computer purchase – and take a good look at where your money is going.

- STEP 2: FRUGAL VERSUS FRIVOLOUS. Do you have a healthy surplus or are you only just scraping by? If you find yourself going into the red, look at the areas where you can alter your spending patterns. Cut down on frivolous expenses: catch the bus instead of a cab and start borrowing books and magazines from the library instead of buying them, for instance.

- STEP 3: SAVVY SAVINGS. Saving a proportion of your income is a great habit to get into. Once you've worked out your weekly budget, you will know how much you can afford to save each week. For the most effective results, organize it so that your financial institution puts a certain amount every week or month into a separate account for you. Pick an interest-bearing account that does not have any ATM cards or credit cards attached to it – you don't want to be able to get at that money. If you do this, if you "pay yourself" first, it becomes a part of your regular budget. You don't have a chance to spend that money, and will end up building a healthy nest egg.

- STEP 4: DON'T DIP. Your budget should include giving yourself a certain amount to spend each week. Stick to that amount. If you run out, that's it for the week – don't dip into your savings.

Like the goddesses of yesteryear, modern-day goddesses have a natural spirit of adventure. Not only do they want to try new experiences on their home turf – they also love the idea of venturing beyond borders and sampling life away from home. Ever fancied the idea of trekking in Nepal or catching the view from the Eiffel Tower? Visiting a new place is always rewarding, and it's exciting just planning your trip and booking the tickets. However, just as Artemis the goddess of hunters made sure she was prepared for her adventures in the wilderness, so you also need to think hard about your travel plans.

Planning and people. Pick your destination carefully. No matter how much you like the idea of adventure, there's no point booking a trip to deepest darkest Africa if you can't even handle camping in your own back yard. Similarly, if you're going to be on the road, sharing rooms and confined to small spaces, choose your traveling companions carefully – make sure get along, or you'll start off as friends and end up as enemies.

Up, up and away. Extended hours on a plane can play havoc with your body clock. As soon as you leave home, try to switch over to your destination's time schedule. If it's nighttime where you're flying, try to sleep. While you're on the plane, drink plenty of water. You might be tempted to ration your liquid intake to avoid those pesky visits to those minuscule toilets, but it's important to stay hydrated if you're on a plane for such a long period of time.

Comfort versus glamor. Be sensible with what you pack. If you're going hiking in the Grand Canyon, leave your Italian slingbacks at home. You can still look like a glamour goddess even if you don't have a wardrobe full of your favorite outfits in tow. Just bring a few cool accessories and wow everyone with your gorgeous smile.

Opening yourself up to new experiences is a stimulating part of life. There's a whole world out there full of new people, exotic cultures and memorable sights. And the best part is that it's just waiting to be discovered. Goddesses know that even though there's no place like home, the adventures and potential that lie beyond what's familiar are part of the abundance life has to offer.

A QUESTION OF BALANCE

Being able to appreciate all the wonderful things life has to offer can only happen if everything is in balance, particularly in your work and your personal life. If you're a go-getting career goddess, it's natural to want to put a lot of time and effort into your work. However, becoming too obsessed with your job means there's a risk you'll neglect other priorities.

This applies to other areas of life, too. Perhaps you're spending a lot of time socializing or, at the other end of the spectrum, holed up at home reading. If your schedule seems to be skewed toward one particular activity, or if it is simply so jampacked that you don't have time for yourself, you need to reassess how to allocate your time.

Balancing your work, friends, family, and personal interests is a key factor in maintaining a healthy outlook. Besides, why limit yourself to experiencing one area of life when there is so much richness you can enjoy if you open yourself up to other possibilities?

The cycle of happiness

When you get into the habit of appreciating all that life has to offer, and reminding yourself of all the positive things that are happening – rather than the negative ones – you'll find yourself realizing how lucky you really are. Looking at the big picture, you'll discover that you have a lot to be thankful for.

Modern-day goddesses realize that this good fortune can be shared around. When you know how great it feels to be happy, you want others to be able to experience the same thing. Just as the mythical goddesses helped the earth – like Athena with her protective spirit and Demeter with her abundant provisions – you can also help the people around you.

Goddesses know that when they're blessed with life's abundance, it's fruitful to give back. This can take many forms, from something as simple as a kind word to a stranger or doing a favor for a friend to volunteering at your local community center or contributing financially to a charity.

It's completely up to you to figure out how you want to give back to society. And rest assured that you'll reap the rewards of making a difference to other people's lives. At the very least, you'll be creating a cycle of happiness and positivity that will have a wonderful impact on your world.

Everyday rituals
for modern-day goddesses

~ Stay true to your values and fundamental
beliefs about life.
~ Listen to your inner voice and trust your intuition.
~ Identify your goals and commit to doing something small each day to help you move one step
closer to what you want to achieve.
~ Look after your body – all goddesses need good
nutrition and a healthy lifestyle.
~ Respect other people if you expect the same thing
in return. Even better, spend time motivating them
and supporting their goals and dreams.
~ Dedicate time to yourself, time when you can be
alone to reflect; give yourself a chance to listen to
your own deepest needs.
~ Be proactive about overcoming your challenges,
and meditate on all the things you can be thankful
for instead of dwelling on what's wrong.

Your personal goddess journey

The key to an abundant life full of happiness, passion, and prosperity lies in your attitude. Health, wealth, and happiness are not thrust upon you, but they are there for the taking – it's up to you to reach for them. That means taking steps to improve your career prospects, control your finances, nurture fulfilling relationships and reap the benefits of a healthy lifestyle.

For example, if you want prosperity, the first thing you need to do is make wise decisions about your money and commit to a regular savings plan.

For a life full of passion, listen to your inner desires and follow your dreams. But remember, you will only succeed in this when you work out a practical action plan to accomplish your goals.

And for a life full of happiness, you first need to have great belief in yourself. Fundamentally, you need to know – and stick to – your personal values. It's the first step to leading a life of integrity.

Your goddess journey can be an exciting path packed with wonderful and rewarding experiences. And the best part is that you're in the driver's seat – you can shape your future and turn your dreams into reality. It may seem scary to have so much responsibility, but wouldn't you prefer to shape the course of your life yourself than let it be dictated by circumstance?

Draw on your inner strength, trust your goddess instincts and embark on an adventure that's set to deliver a fulfilling life – a life full of abundance.

Remember, if you have the right attitude and a practical proactive approach, you can have a life of joy, health, love, and prosperity. Get ready to fulfill your potential, give yourself permission to dream, and enjoy your personal goddess journey!

Published in 2003 by Lansdowne Publishing Pty Ltd
Level 1, 18 Argyle Street, Sydney NSW 2000, Australia

First published in the United States in 2003 by
Red Wheel/Weiser LLC
York Beach, ME
With offices at:
368 Congress Street
Boston, MA 02210
www.redwheelweiser.com

Commissioned by Deborah Nixon
Text: Valerie Khoo
Illustrations: Sue Ninham
Design: Sue Rawkins
Copy Editor: Sarah Shrubb
Production Manager: Sally Stokes
Project Coordinator: Kate Merrifield

ISBN 1-59003-056-7

Set in Stone Serif, Skia, Fontesque, and Fashion on QuarkXPress
Printed in Singapore by Tien Wah Press (Pte) Ltd